TABERNACLE PRAYER

BY *JOHN* *BUGG*

PRESS

Dedicated to the two most amazing people on the planet:

My wife, Mary
And my daughter, Marquette

You are my greatest loves
and my richest treasures on earth.

TABLE OF CONTENTS

PREFACE

For most of my life, I've struggled with prayer. I know I should pray, but I've found it almost impossible to maintain any consistency. While in college as a "ministerial student," there was a period of time when I got up at six in the morning to literally spend time on my knees. (I was very disciplined back then.) I nearly broke my own arm patting myself on the back, but it didn't last long – a few months or maybe a semester. Despite the zeal and willpower of youth, I soon gave it up. I chalked it up as another failure to be the spiritual giant I thought I should be.

In the years since, I've dabbled in prayer. There have been periods of time when I connected with God on a regular basis and truly sensed His presence in my daily life. During those times, prayer was more like a conversation and God was my companion. Once again however, those times were sporadic (actually erratic is a better word for it). When they came along, they were sweet and meaningful, but they never seemed to last very long.

Once I became a pastor, I began leading weekly prayer meetings and offering public prayers that sounded "pastoral." Still, my confidence in prayer remained weak. Does it really make any difference? Why bother to pray if God already knows what I need (and what I'll ask) even before I pray? He'll do what's best anyway, won't He? As a result of my failures and questions, I developed a Huck Finn mentality about prayer.

> ... [Miss Watson] told me to pray every day, and whatever I asked for I would get it. But it warn't so. I tried it. Once I got a fish-line, but no hooks. It warn't any good to me without hooks. I tried for the hooks three or four times, but somehow I couldn't make it work. By and by, one day, I asked Miss Watson to try for me, but she said I was a fool. She never told me why, and I couldn't make it out no way. I set down one time back in the woods, and had a long think about it. I says to myself, if a body can get anything they pray for, why don't Deacon Winn get back the money he lost on pork? Why can't the widow get back her silver snuffbox that was stole? Why

can't Miss Watson fat up? No, says I to
my self, there ain't nothing in it.[1]

That was the state of things until God revealed a
new way to look at prayer and a new way to go about
it. I'm sure this "revelation" is nothing new, but it's
definitely changed my prayer life. It began with a
simple thought: prayer is the relationship. Prayer
is the relationship! We love to talk about having a
personal relationship with God. Prayer is where that
relationship happens. In fact, it *is* the relationship.
We talk to God and sometimes He talks back. In
the process, we grow closer to Him. Prayer isn't so
much about getting answers or changing outcomes,
it's simply the basic way we interact with God. Of
course, there are times when we ask and He answers,
but I'm convinced that's *not* the primary purpose of
prayer. I've come to believe that the primary purpose
of prayer is just to spend time with Him, getting to
know Him and, hopefully, becoming more like Him.

Along with this new understanding of prayer,
God revealed a method of prayer based on the Old
Testament Tabernacle. For lack of a better term, I call
it Tabernacle Prayer. I haven't counted myself, but I
read somewhere that there are more chapters devoted
to the Tabernacle than the number of chapters in any

of the four Gospels. Wow! In comparison to only two chapters on creation, that's an awful lot of paper and ink devoted to the construction of a tent, don't you think? Maybe there's more than meets the eye.

Studies I've seen on the Tabernacle often deal with the symbols of Christ found in it. While I have no doubt that His fingerprint is all over the blueprint of the Tabernacle, the Tabernacle is more than just a foreshadowing of the person and work of Christ. I believe the Tabernacle is actually a pattern for prayer – a road map to intimacy with God. After all, this was the place the Israelites met with God during their journey from Egypt to the Promised Land. Isn't it also possible (or even likely) that the Tabernacle describes how we meet with God during our own journey through life?

After these "revelations," I began using the Tabernacle as my prayer guide. For the first time in my life, I'm excited about prayer and look forward to it. Prayer is no longer a duty; it's an interactive experience. Using holy imagination, I am learning how to walk the Tabernacle path to the Holy of Holies. Along the way, every physical sense is engaged – sight, sound, smell, taste, and touch. And better yet, each walk along the path is unique. I see new things, hear new things, and experience new things. Best of all, prayer is no longer a duty. It's actually enjoyable.

It's my sincere prayer that this book will transform your prayer life and your life in general. There's no greater joy than being in a relationship with the most incredible person in the universe – the Creator Himself. Prayer is how we go about it. In the words of the Psalmist, I pray that the words of this book and the meditation of your hearts in its pages will be acceptable and pleasing to God, our Rock and our Redeemer.

John A. Bugg
February 5, 2014

INTRODUCTION

I n protestant theology, there's a concept called the priesthood of believers. The apostle Peter was perhaps the first to use that terminology. Writing during the first century, Peter described the early Christians as "a chosen race, *a royal priesthood*, a holy nation, a people for his own possession" (1 Peter 2:9 ESV). Simply stated, the priesthood of believers means that every believer has immediate access to the throne room of God. There are no barriers and no locked doors between the believer and God. At any given moment day or night, we can speak with our Heavenly Father. While God will not hear our prayers if we fail to confess our sins (*see*, Psalm 66:18 and Isaiah 59:1-2), access to Him is never denied. By virtue of the finished work of Christ, we have the right to approach God at any time. In fact, the writer of Hebrews encourages us to make use of that privilege, "Let us therefore come boldly to the throne of grace, that we may obtain mercy and find grace to help in time of need." (Hebrews 4:16 KJV).

The right to approach God, however, doesn't mean that we can (or should) approach Him any way we want. The fact that we have instant access doesn't mean we have the right to barge into His presence like a UPS guy just to drop off our requests and be on our way. While there are times when a sudden crisis compels us to rush into the throne room, most often our "need" just isn't that urgent. Most of the time, we should approach God with the reverence that is rightfully due Him. Like the Old Testament priests, we should approach Him carefully (even cautiously) out of respect for who He is. Like the Old Testament priests, we should follow the pathway to His presence laid out in the design of the Tabernacle.

The Courtyard Walls

Exodus 38:9-17 (HCSB) *⁹ Then he made the courtyard. The hangings on the south side of the courtyard were of finely spun linen, 150 feet in length, ¹⁰ including their 20 posts and 20 bronze bases. The hooks and bands of the posts were silver. ¹¹ The hangings on the north side were also 150 feet in length, including their 20 posts and 20 bronze bases. The hooks and bands of the posts were silver. ¹² The hangings on the west side were 75 feet in length, including their 10 posts and 10 bases. The hooks and bands of the posts were silver. ¹³ The hangings on the east toward the sunrise were also 75 feet in length. ¹⁴ The hangings on one side of the gate were 22½ feet, including their three posts and three bases. ¹⁵ It was the same for the other side. The hangings were 22½ feet, including their three posts and three bases on both sides of the courtyard gate. ¹⁶ All the hangings around the courtyard were of finely spun linen. ¹⁷ The bases for the posts were bronze; the hooks and bands of the posts were silver; and the plating for the tops of the posts was silver. All the posts of the courtyard were banded with silver.*

CHAPTER 1

PULLING THE CURTAINS OF SECRECY

A s you approach the Tabernacle grounds, the first structure you encounter is actually a fence made of white linen panels. Approximately 7½ feet tall, the panels enclose a rectangular courtyard measuring 150 feet by 75 feet. They literally fence out the world from the holy grounds. They remind us of the need to "be still and know that He is God" (Psalm 46:10). They also serve to teach us the secret to prayer shared by Jesus in the Sermon on the Mount (Matthew 6:5-8) and in His private prayer life (Matthew 14:23; Mark 1:35; Mark 6:46; Luke 5:16; Luke 6:12; John 6:15). The secret to prayer is secret prayer, taking time out of our "busy" day to meet alone with Him. Secret prayer requires stillness, solitude and silence. So SSH! Slow down. Shut out. Hush up.

Slow Down (Stillness)

"Be still, and know that I am God; I will be exalted among the nations, I will be exalted in the earth." Psalm 46:10 (ESV)

We live in a world that moves at breakneck speed. Our culture is described in an old Eagles song as "life in the fast lane" and we truly are just about to lose our minds. Part of the secret to prayer is learning to slow down and be still. Otherwise, we'll become conformed to the world and its pace. Being still provides God the opportunity to transform us and renew our minds (Romans 12:2).

Stillness also fosters proper reverence and respect for God. Relationships take time and our relationship with God is certainly no different. In the words of Richard Foster, we will never have time for prayer; we must make time.[2] We love to think of God as our friend, but if we spent as little time with our earthly friends as we do with Him, those friendships wouldn't last long. In a similar way, we disrespect God when we approach Him in a rush and fail to spend quality time with Him.

John Ortberg once sought the advice of a mentor about improving his spiritual health. The mentor provided some unexpected wisdom that was actually very simple. He said, "You must ruthlessly eliminate hurry from your life." Ortberg's conclusion? We all suffer from "hurry sickness," a disease that wrecks havoc in our spiritual lives.

> Hurry is the great enemy of spiritual life in our day. Hurry can destroy our souls... Again and again, as we pursue spiritual life, we must do battle with hurry. For many of us, the great danger is not that we will renounce our faith. It is that we will become so distracted and rushed and preoccupied that we will settle for a mediocre version of it.[3]

Stillness is the antidote to hurry sickness. It's a prerequisite to intimacy with God, because "love and hurry are fundamentally incompatible."[4]

So as we begin our time of Tabernacle prayer, we remember the walls surrounding the Tabernacle courtyard. They remind us to "cease striving," another translation of "be still" from Psalm 46:10. I like that translation. Cease striving! Stop struggling! Quit flailing around! Just slow yourself down and be still for a minute or two. Know that He is God and you don't have to be. Let that knowledge bring you peace in a world that's spinning out of control.

Shut Out (Solitude)

"And when you pray, you must not be like the hypocrites. For they love to stand and pray in the synagogues and at the street corners, that they may be seen by others. Truly, I say to you, they have received their reward. But when you pray, go into your room and shut the door and pray to your Father who is in secret. And your Father who sees in secret will reward you." Matthew 6:5-6 (ESV)

In the Sermon on the Mount, Jesus taught that spiritual practices should be done "in secret." Specifically with respect to prayer, Jesus told His disciples to go into an inner room (or closet) and shut the door. Praying in secret like this serves two purposes. First, secret prayer preempts the pride in us that seeks the approval of others as in "Hey, look at me. I'm praying." But maybe just as important, the solitude of secret prayer forces us to shut out the world and just be alone with God.

The Tabernacle had multiple walls, which teach a similar lesson about solitude. To reach the presence of God in the Holy of Holies, the priest would pass through three sets of walls – the walls of the court-yard, the Holy Place, and the Holy of Holies. Once in the presence of God, those same walls separated the priest from the rest of the world.

One advantage to solitude is that it allows us to avoid the harmful effects of the rat race. An experiment was done with mice some years ago to determine the harmful effects of group conformity. They discovered that it takes a very high dose of amphetamines to kill a mouse living in solitude. But a dose twenty times smaller is lethal to a group of mice. The reason? When mice are in a group, they agitate one another. One starts hopping around and the others get hyped up, too. In fact, if a mouse given no amphetamines is placed in a group who have, that mouse will be dead within ten minutes.[5] That's how deadly the rat race can be. Solitude is necessary because it's "the one place on earth where we can escape the forces of society that will otherwise relentlessly mold us."[6]

The greatest advantage to solitude, however, is the fact that it creates space so that God can speak to us. Name just about any famous character in the Bible and God spoke to them when they were alone. Check it out for yourself – Abraham (Genesis 12), Jacob (Genesis 32), Moses (Exodus 3), Joshua (Joshua 1), Gideon (Judges 6), Samuel (1 Samuel 3), Elijah (1 Kings 19), Isaiah (Isaiah 6) Jonah (Jonah 2),

Zechariah (Luke 1), Mary the mother of Jesus (Luke 1), Peter (Acts 10) and John (Revelation 1). Does anybody else see a pattern here? God is everywhere and He can speak whenever He wants, but it's no coincidence that He often chose to speak to people in the Bible when they were alone.

The Tabernacle walls remind us to shut out the world and just spend time alone with God. By doing so, we escape the whirlwind of constant demands. God said as much in Isaiah 26:20, "Come, my people, enter your chambers, and shut your doors behind you; hide yourselves for a little while until the fury has passed by" (Isaiah 26:20 (ESV). In that setting, we have a chance to hear God speak.

Hush Up (Silence)

"And when you pray, do not heap up empty phrases as the Gentiles do, for they think that they will be heard for their many words. Do not be like them, for your Father knows what you need before you ask him." Matthew 6:7-8 (ESV)

Another aspect of secret prayer is the practice of silence. Will Rogers once said, "Never miss a good chance to shut up." That statement is so true when it comes to the subject of prayer. When we're silent, God has a chance to get a word in.

Continuing His teaching on secret prayer, Jesus specifically discouraged repetition or empty words. Why? Because your Father already knows what you need before you even ask Him. Make no mistake. God wants us to talk to Him about everything and Scripture encourages us to present our requests to Him in prayer. But sometimes, the most powerful and intimate communication takes place when no one says a word. Just ask any young couple you catch staring into each other's eyes.

In times of silence, we commune with God. We enjoy the Other. We focus our attention solely on the object of our love. Silence brings meaning and depth to the relationship. It fosters trust in God and endears our affections for Him. Jesus said the Father would reward us when we pray in secret. In fact, He *is* the reward! When we stop talking and turn off the other voices in our lives, God's presence fills the silence.

Most of us know the story of the day God spoke to Elijah. At least we know a phrase from that story. We know that God spoke "in a still, small voice." It may be helpful to read it again, so here it is from 1 Kings 19:9-12 (NKJV).

⁹ And there he [Elijah] went into a cave, and spent the night in that place; and behold, the word of the Lord came to him, and He said to him, "What are you doing here, Elijah?"

¹⁰ So he said, "I have been very zealous for the Lord God of hosts; for the children of Israel have forsaken Your covenant, torn down Your altars, and killed Your prophets with the sword. I alone am left; and they seek to take my life."

¹¹ Then He said, "Go out, and stand on the mountain before the Lord." And behold, the Lord passed by, and a great and strong wind tore into the mountains and broke the rocks in pieces before the Lord, but the Lord was not in the wind; and after the wind an earthquake, but the Lord was not in the earthquake; ¹² and after the earthquake a fire, but the Lord was not in the fire; and after the fire a still small voice.

The phrase translated "still small voice" is actually subject to different interpretations. The ESV translates it: "the sound of a low whisper." The NASB translates it: "the sound of a gentle blowing." And the NIV translates it: "a gentle whisper." A very literal translation is "the voice of sheer silence." I like the "sound" of that a lot. Sheer silence has a voice. We've all heard it. God speaks to us in the silence.

Summary

The Tabernacle walls teach us many important lessons about prayer. They remind us of the need to slow down or "be still" in the presence God. They teach us to shut out the world and enjoy being alone with God. They teach us that God fills the silence if we'll just be quiet in His presence. This is a great way to start your prayers. Give God a few minutes of still, solitary silence. Make time for it because if you don't have time for stillness and solitude and silence, you probably don't have time for God.

Practical Suggestions

At the conclusion of each chapter, I will offer some practical suggestions about how to apply the preceding content. My prayer is that God will use these suggestions to stimulate your "holy imagination," as you walk the Tabernacle path of prayer into God's presence. (These suggestions are collected in the Appendix.)

- Pick a time and place for secret prayer and stick to it. Wherever and whenever it is, God will make it sacred.

- Do whatever is necessary to avoid interruption or distraction – shut the door, close the curtains, turn off the computer, silence the phone, etc. (You'll soon learn what needs to be done because the first few times you'll probably be interrupted and/or distracted.)

- Remember the lessons of the Tabernacle walls – stillness, solitude and silence.

- Begin with Scripture. Read, recite, or just recall a verse that helps you settle yourself and get focused. For example, Psalm 46:10 or Isaiah 40:31.

- As you begin the season of prayer, envision the white linen walls of the Tabernacle courtyard. Imagine pulling them around you like curtains, shutting out the distractions of the world. Listen for the sheer sound of silence.

- You'll know it's time to move on when you experience "the peace of God which passes understanding." At that point, proceed to the gate.

The Gate

Exodus 38:18-20 (HCSB) *18 The screen for the gate of the courtyard was embroidered with blue, purple, and scarlet yarn, and finely spun linen. It was 30 feet long, and like the hangings of the courtyard, 7½ feet high. 19 It had four posts, including their four bronze bases. Their hooks were silver, and the bands as well as the plating of their tops were silver. 20 All the tent pegs for the tabernacle and for the surrounding courtyard were bronze.*

CHAPTER 2

ENTERING THE GATE

H ave you heard the one about the auto mechanic who decided to help out the local ministers? One day a Catholic priest brought his car into the mechanic's shop for repairs. When the work was done, the priest reached for his wallet to pay for the repairs. The generous mechanic wouldn't take his money. He said, "There's no charge because you're a man of the cloth." When the mechanic came to work the next day, he found a thank you note from the priest and three bottles of fine wine. Some time later, a rabbi brought his car in for repairs. Once again, when the rabbi tried to pay for the work, the mechanic stopped him and said, "You don't owe me a thing because you're a servant of God." The next day when the mechanic arrived for work, there was a thank you note from the rabbi and three dozen bagels. A few more days passed and the mechanic's pastor brought his car in for repairs. When the preacher returned and tried to pay, the mechanic stopped him as he'd done with the priest and the rabbi. He said, "You don't owe me a thing because you're a Baptist preacher and my very own pastor." When the mechanic came to work the next day, guess what he found waiting at the door? Three more Baptist preachers.

Unfortunately, we often treat God like that in our prayers. God pours blessing into our lives and we just keep coming back for more, without ever saying thanks. Remember the time Jesus healed ten lepers? Only one returned to thank Him. I'm afraid that's an accurate reflection of the percentage of time we return thanks to God. Maybe one out of ten times, we remember to thank God for being so generous toward us. Our prayers should include more than "I need" or "I want." We may end up there, but that's not where we should start.

The gate into the Tabernacle teaches us how to avoid treating God like a genie in a bottle. It reminds us of the proper way to approach God and the reason we can approach Him at all. I'll spell it out for you – G.A.T.E. The "G" stands for give. The "A" for adore. The "T" for take. And the "E" for enter.

Give Thanks for His Actions

Enter His gates with thanksgiving and His courts with praise. Give thanks to Him and praise His name. Psalm 100:4 (HCSB)

Psalm 100:4 describes the proper way to approach God in prayer – with thanksgiving and praise. There is a difference between thanksgiving and praise. Thanksgiving is for the gift. Praise is for the Giver. We thank God for what He does. We praise Him for who He is. One focuses on His actions and the other focuses on His attributes.

In *The Screwtape Letters*, C. S. Lewis described a fictional world where one demon was training another demon in the art of temptation and trial. The book is actually a series of letters from a demon named Screwtape to his protégé, Wormwood, in which Screwtape provides advice based on his years of experience. In one of the letters, Screwtape advises Wormwood to plant seeds of discouragement because Screwtape had discovered they almost always grew into doubt or hopelessness. When Wormwood asked why the practice wasn't always fruitful, Screwtape said he'd found that seeds of discouragement won't grow in a thankful heart.

That's one reason to begin prayer with thanksgiving. It's a defense against discouragement. As we remember what He's done for us and thank Him for His many gifts, we actually fill up the space in our hearts where despair can live. Thanksgiving crowds out the disappointments of the day and the "woefulness" of our week.

A better reason for thanksgiving is simply that God deserves it. As children, we were taught to say "thank you" when someone did something nice, even if it was a common courtesy like opening a door for us. Doesn't God deserve the same? We need to thank God for what He's done and all the gifts He's given us. Perhaps that's why the psalmist said we should enter His gates with thanksgiving.

Adore His Attributes

Not only does Psalm 100:4 tell us to give thanks, it also says we should "enter His courts with praise." After thanking God for what He's done, we praise Him for who He is. We express adoration for His attributes.

One of my all time favorite books is *The Knowledge of the Holy* by A. W. Tozer. It's a short book about the "contemporary" need for a more lofty view of God. (I put quotes around "contemporary" because the book was written in the 1950s.) Using short chapters, Tozer writes about different attributes of God. But don't let the brevity of the chapters fool you. Each one is much deeper than it is long. To name a few, Tozer writes about God's faithfulness, His goodness, His love, His grace and His holiness. These are some of the things we praise Him for. We praise Him for just being who He is.

All of us like to receive praise. We feel loved when someone praises us. In fact, "words of affirmation" is one of the five love languages – five ways we express love to one another.[7] In that respect, praise is saying "I love you" to God. More than that, praise is telling God why we love Him and what it is we love about Him.

In reality, God doesn't need our praise or even our love for that matter. He's sufficient in Himself. Our praise doesn't bolster His confidence or improve His self-image. He can do without it. But we can't! We need to praise someone bigger than ourselves. We need to be reminded that God is awesome. We also need the practice for the day we arrive in heaven.

Take Time to Worship

But You are holy, enthroned on the praises of Israel. Psalm 22:3 (HCSB)

Psalm 22 begins with a familiar passage that Jesus quoted as He hung upon the cross, "My God, My God, why have you forsaken me?" Psalm 22 also contains several verses describing the actual crucifixion of Jesus (*see*, Psalm 22:7-8, 14-18), hundreds of years before it happened. What's even more incredible is that Psalm 22 was written before crucifixion was used as a means of execution. For those reasons, Psalm 22 is an amazing prophetic utterance.

But there's another reason Psalm 22 is amazing. Psalm 22:3 states that God is enthroned on the praises of His people. In the King James version, the word "enthroned" is translated as "inhabits." We enthrone God when we worship. He actually inhabits the praises of His people.

When we come to the gate of the Tabernacle, we enter with thanksgiving and praise. By doing so, we enthrone Him and invite Him to inhabit our praise. We take time to worship because, whether it's coronation or habitation, it takes time for God to take His seat on the throne of our heart or dwell with us.

Imagine that you and I are close friends who haven't seen or spoken to each for years. If I called you up out of the blue one day and asked for a favor, would you grant it? What if I asked for $10,000?

Would you give it to me after a decade of silence from my end? Here's the deal. Far too often we crawl up into the lap of God asking for "favors" when we might not have spoken to Him for a long time.

We must take time to worship even when we have no pressing need. We must take time to worship, because He deserves it. We must take time to worship Him, otherwise we'll end up worshipping someone or something else.

Enter the Gate

> *[7]So Jesus said again, "I assure you: I am the door of the sheep. [8]All who came before Me are thieves and robbers, but the sheep didn't listen to them. [9]I am the door. If anyone enters by Me, he will be saved and will come in and go out and find pasture. [10]A thief comes only to steal and to kill and to destroy. I have come so that they may have life and have it in abundance. John 10:7-10 (HCSB)*

The gate of the tabernacle is described in the book of Exodus: "The gate of the courtyard is to have a thirty-foot screen embroidered with blue, purple, and scarlet yarn, and finely spun linen" (Exodus 27:16 HCSB). The colors are significant because they speak of Christ. The blue speaks of heaven and His divinity. The red speaks of blood (or earth) and His humanity. The white linen background speaks of His purity. And the purple speaks of His royalty. The only reason we have access to God is because Jesus Christ embodies all of these things. He is divine. He was human. He lived a perfect life. And He will always be the King of all Kings.

The colors of the gateway tapestry have also been linked with the four Gospels. Matthew focuses his gospel on Jesus as the King, who came to establish His kingdom. His color is purple. Mark focuses on the Suffering Servant, obedient unto death. His color is red. Luke describes Jesus as the Perfect Man, who came to save us from our sin. His color is white. And John describes Jesus as the divine Son of God sent from heaven. His color is blue.

Regardless of which gospel you read, they all teach that we can approach God because Jesus is the Gate. Both in this life (through prayer) and in the life to come, we can enter the presence of God solely because of who Jesus is and what He's done. As the perfect sacrifice for our sin, Jesus opened the way for us to receive forgiveness. And on the third day, as our risen Savior, He rolled away the final stone that blocked our way – death itself (Romans 6:23).

The gate of the Tabernacle confronts us with a simple truth. No one could enter the Holy Place, much less the Holy of Holies, without going through the gate. Likewise, no one can stand before God in this life or the next, without entering through Jesus Christ.

Thank God! Jesus said, "I am the door." Thank God! He also said, "I am the way, the truth, and the life. No one comes to the father except by Him" (John 14:6 HCSB). We can enter His gates with thanksgiving and His courts with praise because Jesus made a way for us!

Practical Suggestions

Using holy imagination, approach the Tabernacle gate and enter the courtyard.

- Give thanks to God for things He has done for you recently and in the past – opportunities he has given you, people he has placed in your life, circumstances He has orchestrated to bless you, etc. Thank Him for both material and spiritual blessings.

- Praise God by focusing on a favorite attribute of His character. You may even want to read a chapter from Tozer's book, *The Knowledge of the Holy*.

- Take your time. Worship God in spirit and in truth for who He is and what He's done.

- Find a hymnal and worship Him in song. Or, if you know a worship song by memory, sing it from your heart. (*Holy, Holy, Holy* and Chris Tomlin's *How Great Is Our God* are good options.)

- Reflect on Christ in the colors of the gateway tapestry – blue for His divinity, red for His humanity, white for His purity and purple for His royalty.

- After spending time in worship, imagine yourself walking through the gate into the Tabernacle courtyard.

THE BRONZE ALTAR

Exodus 38:1-7 (HCSB) *[1]Bezalel constructed the altar of burnt offering from
acacia wood. It was square, 7½ feet long
and 7½ feet wide, and was 4½ feet high.
[2]He made horns for it on its four corners;
the horns were of one piece. Then he
overlaid it with bronze. [3]He made all the
altar's utensils: the pots, shovels, basins,
meat forks, and firepans; he made all its
utensils of bronze. [4]He constructed for
the altar a grate of bronze mesh under
its ledge, halfway up from the bottom. [5]At
the four corners of the bronze grate he
cast four rings as holders for the poles.
[6]Also, he made the poles of acacia wood
and overlaid them with bronze. [7]Then
he inserted the poles into the rings on
the sides of the altar in order to carry it
with them. He constructed the altar with
boards so that it was hollow.*

CHAPTER 3

LAYING YOUR SACRIFICE ON THE ALTAR

When Veteran's Day rolls around each year, I'm often humbled by the sacrifice of those who have served our country, some of whom have laid down their very lives in the "last full measure of devotion." This year I saw an ESPN compilation of servicemen and women surprising their loved ones when they returned home. The shock and joy of family members, especially the children, was very moving. It was as if they couldn't believe what they were seeing. But when it finally registered, the reactions were price-less – usually a sprint followed by a hug and then tears. It was beautiful to watch. It made me want to stand up and salute them all – the veterans for their willingness to lay their lives on the altar of service and their family members for their willingness to let them do it.

Stepping through the gate and into the Tabernacle courtyard, the first object you would see was an altar. It was a fire pit made of bronze, measuring 7½ feet square and 4½ tall. When in use, no doubt the heat could be felt as you approached. The bronze altar was front and center in the courtyard of the Tabernacle. A hot, visible reminder of human sinfulness. A constant blaze, making the case for God's holiness and our woeful lack thereof. A not-so-gentle reminder that God is a consuming fire. Day after day, week after week, and year after year, the priests would offer animal sacrifices to atone for their sins and the sins of the Israelite people. Blood was shed. Flesh was burned. Guiltless animals were sacrificed on the bronze altar.

What meaning does that bronze altar have for us today? We no longer present animal sacrifices. There's no need. The ultimate sacrifice for all sin – the very Son of God Himself, Jesus Christ – put an end to that for all time and eternity. As the writer of Hebrew put it, "…[H]e has appeared once for all at the culmination of the ages to do away with sin by the sacrifice of himself" (Hebrews 9:26 NIV) and "… we have been made holy through the sacrifice of the body of Jesus Christ once for all" (Hebrews 10:10 NIV). The same thought inspired the apostle John to write, "This is love, not that we loved God, but that He loved us and gave His Son as an atoning sacrifice for our sin" (1 John 4:10 NIV). In view of that incredible Truth, the meaning of the bronze altar for us is something different entirely. It reminds us that, when we pray, we should lay our lives and our love on the altar.

Lay Your Life on the Altar

> [23] *And He was saying to them all, "If anyone wishes to come after Me, he must deny himself, and take up his cross daily and follow Me.* [24] *For whoever wishes to save his life will lose it, but whoever loses his life for My sake, he is the one who will save it." Luke 9:23-24 (NASB)*

Jesus minced no words when he described the requirements for following after Him. In the Luke passage above, Jesus identifies them: deny yourself, take up your cross daily, and follow Me. In prayer, the Tabernacle altar is where we do that.

I'm a belated fan of The Eagles, the rock band of my youth. Back then, I was too puritanical to appreciate them. As I've mellowed with age, I've begun to see the wisdom in their lyrics. In their most famous song of all, *Hotel California*, they decry the trap of modern culture and Western materialism. At one point, they sing, "In the master's chamber, they are gathered for the feast. They stab it with their steely knives, but they just can't kill the beast." I'm not completely sure what in the world that means, but I have an idea. The "steely beast" is the "self" that Jesus said we must deny. On the Tabernacle altar, we stab it with our steely knives. The beast is in me and, in truth, it *is* me. I must put it to death daily. I must submit my "self" to the knife of a loving Father and surrender it to death. This is self-denial in prayer. It is laying my very life at His disposal.

The apostle Paul understood this. In fact, on at least two different occasions, he wrote about it. In Romans chapter 12, after eloquently describing the wonder and beauty of the gospel, Paul put it this way: "I beseech you therefore, brethren, by the mercies of God, that you present your bodies a living sacrifice, holy and acceptable to God, which is your reasonable service" (Romans 12:1 NKJV). I like that translation of the passage because it describes our daily sacrifice as a reasonable service. We shouldn't do any less. In view of God's mercies, it's only *reasonable* that we would lay our life on the altar of sacrifice and service. That's what a proper understanding of His grace evokes in us. First, His grace overwhelms us. Then, it compels us.

Paul put it differently in Galatians 2:20 (NASB): "I have been crucified with Christ; and it is no longer I who live, but Christ lives in me; and the life which I now live in the flesh I live by faith in the Son of God, who loved me and gave Himself up for me." In other words, Paul considered himself a dead man. His life belonged to Someone else. It was commandeered by Christ Himself. Paul no longer lived for "self." Having laid his life on the altar, Paul lived for Christ and by faith in Christ.

Our servicemen and women lay down their lives for people they don't even know. At the alter, we lay down our lives for Someone we *do* know. We sacrifice our "self" to Him so that we don't lose our lives in pursuit of a lesser life. It's not easy, but it's reasonable because that Someone died to bring us grace.

Lay Your Love on the Altar

> [28] *One of the teachers of the law came and heard them debating. Noticing that Jesus had given them a good answer, he asked him, "Of all the commandments, which is the most important?"* [29] *"The most important one," answered Jesus, "is this:*

'Hear, O Israel: The Lord our God, the Lord is one. [30] Love the Lord your God with all your heart and with all your soul and with all your mind and with all your strength.'" Mark 12:28-30 (NIV)

When asked which was the most important commandment of all, Jesus had a simple answer. He said it was the command to love God with everything – all our heart, soul, mind and strength. Those who asked the question weren't even surprised by His answer. They agreed with it, perhaps because it doesn't even need to be written down. Somewhere in the human psyche, we *know* that God exists. The enemy of our souls and the philosophies of each age have sought to ignore it or deny it, but human beings are born with an innate desire to love and worship the God who made us, even if it comes at great personal cost.

No one knew this better than Abraham, the father of faith. After being promised the moon and the stars (or at least descendants as numerous), Abraham was put to the test. God asked Abraham to sacrifice the one thing on earth that he loved most. Incredibly, God asked Abraham to sacrifice Isaac, the very son God had promised and through whom God planned to bless the world. Personally, I cringe at this story in Genesis

22. It seems so cruel. How could a loving God do such a thing? Why would He ask so much? Our mistake is thinking that He doesn't still. That's the essence of the greatest commandment. God commands us to love Him most and to love Him with all we are.

God's request of Abraham was extreme. But the wonder of the story is that Abraham's obedience was no less extreme. He tried to go through with it. He took Isaac to the mountain God had named for the sacrifice. He dismissed the servants who might have stopped him from sacrificing Isaac. He even made it past the awful question asked by Isaac himself, "Dad, here's the wood and the fire, but where's the lamb?" (Genesis 22:7 author's paraphrase). Yeah, I know. The next verse records Abraham telling Isaac that God Himself would provide the lamb (Genesis 22:8). Maybe Abraham actually believed that. But maybe not. The writer of Hebrews suggests that Abraham believed something even greater. According to Hebrews 11:19, Abraham believed that God could raise the dead. Fortunately, the story ends well. Isaac is spared at the last second. God intervenes to stop Abraham. And God does indeed provide a lamb as a substitute for Isaac.

So how can God ask us to love Him that much? Above everything else and everyone else in our lives? I think it's because He expects no less of us than He was (and is) willing to give Himself. He loves us individually, wholeheartedly, and unconditionally. We know this because the story didn't end so well for the Son of another promise. One day, the promised Messiah – God's One and Only Son – offered Himself as a sacrifice. Like Abraham, Jesus obeyed the Father's terrible request. Like Isaac, Jesus trusted His Father. But this time the hammer fell, driving spikes into the hands and feet of Christ. His flesh was torn and His blood was shed so that we could be forgiven. His story ended in death. Well almost. Amazingly, Abraham's faith was well-founded. God is able to raise the dead. On the third day, God's love outlived death itself. On the third day, Christ arose.

There are many lessons in the story of Abraham and Isaac. The basic one is this. Abraham was willing to lay his greatest love and his greatest hope on the altar. We must do the same and lay our love on the altar of sacrifice. We offer all our heart – our greatest loves and affections. We offer all our soul – the part of us that exercises freedom of choice. We offer all our mind – our thoughts and our thought life. We offer all our strength – our body itself for His service. Like Abraham, we express our love for God by holding nothing back from the altar. We acknowledge that God has first dibs on everything.

The altar is the place we express our unconditional love toward God. At the altar we sacrifice heart, soul, mind and strength. We tell God that He owns all of us and can do whatever He wants with us. At the altar, we join the prayer of Jesus in the Garden of Gethsemane: "Not my will, but Thine be done."

Summary

The bronze altar of the Tabernacle was a necessary step in the approach to God. Like the gate, no one could enter the Holy Place or Holy of Holies, without a stop at the altar. We try to skip this part of prayer. We want to get to the throne room so we can enjoy God's presence and ask for stuff. But prayer is lifeless without it. Unless we lay our lives and our love on the altar, we forfeit the rest of the trip. We miss the victory of surrender and the joy of submission.

Practical Suggestions

Using holy imagination, approach the bronze altar slowly and reverently.

- Feel the heat of God's holiness and the warmth of His love.

- Deny yourself. Present your body as a living sacrifice. Maybe even say aloud, "I am crucified with Christ."

- Express your love for God and offer Him your affections, your decisions, your thought life and your physical strength. Lovingly surrender yourself to Him. Submit to His will.

- Ask God to help you fully yield yourself. Ask Him to increase your love for Him.

THE BRONZE LAVER

Exodus 30:17-21 (HCSB) *[17] The Lord spoke to Moses: [18] "Make a bronze basin for washing and a bronze stand for it. Set it between the tent of meeting and the altar, and put water in it. [19] Aaron and his sons must wash their hands and feet from the basin. [20] Whenever they enter the tent of meeting or approach the altar to minister by burning up an offering to the Lord, they must wash with water so that they will not die. [21] They must wash their hands and feet so that they will not die; this is to be a permanent statute for them, for Aaron and his descendants throughout their generations."*

Exodus 38:8 (HCSB) *[8] He made the bronze basin and its stand from the bronze mirrors of the women who served at the entrance to the tent of meeting.*

Chapter 4

Confessing Your Sin

A ndy Cook tells a story on himself in one of his books. It involved a borrowed pitchfork that fell out of the truck he was driving and onto a busy street. When he circled back and stopped at a stop sign just a few feet away from the "scene of the crime," he saw that two drivers had stopped to remove the hazard. They were on the side of the road with the pitchfork. At that point, Andy had a decision to make. I'll let him tell it from there in his own words.

> "If only they'd leave," I thought. "If they'd only walk away, I'd grab that fork and run. No one would know."
>
> They didn't leave quickly enough and the traffic behind me was pushing me to make a decision. Turn right, and I would

go right past Mr. and Ms. Safety, and they'd spot me. Turn right, and I'd have to apologize and sheepishly reclaim the instrument of my wrongdoing. Turn right, and I might have to pay for damage done, though I could see no damage. Turn right, and I'd certainly have to endure a lecture.

The car behind me demanded a decision.

I turned left.[8]

All of us have a tendency to "turn left." We run from our mistakes and hide from our guilt. Like criminals, even if we're caught red-handed, we plead not guilty and challenge someone to prove otherwise. We know the truth about ourselves, but are reluctant to face it. As a result, we walk around with unconfessed sin and unresolved guilt.

When it comes to prayer, ignoring our sin isn't an option. If we want to stand in the presence of God, we must deal with it. That's the lesson of the bronze laver. The laver (think lavatory) was where the priests washed up before entering the Holy Place. It was (and still is) a necessary stop on the way to intimacy with God. The Psalmist understood this: "Who may ascend the hill of the Lord? And who may stand in His holy place? He who has clean hands and a pure heart,…"

(Psalm 24:3-4). Before we can stand in the presence of the Holy One, we must see ourselves for who we are and see our sin for what it is. You'll "C" what I mean.

Consequences of Sin

If I regard [cherish] iniquity in my heart,
The Lord will not hear. Psalm 66:18 (NKJV)

Behold, the Lord's hand is not so short
that it cannot save; nor is His ear so dull
that it cannot hear. But your iniquities
have made a separation between you and
your God, and your sins have hidden His
face from you so that He does not hear.
Isaiah 59:1-2 (NASB)

Our reluctance to face up to our sinfulness and to seek cleansing from our sins has devastating consequences far beyond the burden of guilt we carry. According to Psalm 66:18, when we allow iniquity to remain in our heart, we plug the ears of God to our prayers. We end up talking to ourselves because God stops listening. Wow! That's a scary thought. God won't hear us if we coddle our sin, cherishing it in our hearts.

Perhaps Psalm 66:18 refers only to habitual sin – sin we refuse to evict from our hearts. Rather than addressing it, we treat it like a household pet. You know, the kind of sin we feed with our thought life. The sin we dote on, even when it makes a mess. We think to ourselves, it'll eventually be house-trained and, in the meantime, it's not so bad.

Maybe that's the kind of sin the psalmist said would deafen God. Maybe, but is it worth the risk? Especially when you consider the companion passage in Isaiah 59:1-2. According to Isaiah, refusing to deal with sin not only closes God's ears, it separates us from God. It causes Him to hide His face from us. Even worse, it "shortens His hand." He'd love to help us but He can't reach that far. There's something in the way called iniquity.

The bottom line: sin has consequences beyond the guilt we may feel or the damage it may do to our lives on earth. Harboring sin, habitual or otherwise, isolates us from God. It places us beyond His reach. No wonder the laver stood at the entrance to the Holy Place.

Conviction of Sin

²³ Search me, O God, and know my heart; try me, and know my thoughts. ²⁴ And see if there be any wicked way in me, and lead me in the way everlasting. Psalm 139:23-4 (KJV)

The Scripture provides no dimensions for the bronze laver. It does, however, tell us how it was made. It was made from the bronze mirrors of the women who served at the entrance to the tent of meeting (Exodus 38:8). Filled with water, the laver was a huge mirror. Anyone who stepped up and looked down would see their own reflection.

The Holy Spirit now performs the same function in our lives. He holds a mirror up so we can see ourselves and become convicted of sin (John 16:8). But we must participate in the process. How? By praying with the psalmist, "Search me, O God, and know my heart; try me, and know my thoughts. See if there is any wicked way in me, then lead me in the everlasting way" (Psalm 139:23-24 NKJV). In other words, we ask God to examine of our hearts and reveal our wickedness so that He can straighten us out. We expose ourselves to His search so that we can find our way back to the right track.

I read about a former Jack in the Box manager named Thomas Martin. One night just before closing time, the restaurant was robbed and the thief got away with $307. As part of the investigation, Mr. Martin provided a sketch artist with a detailed description of the thief. After completing the sketch, the artist observed that the person looked an awful lot like

Mr. Martin. When the investigators also noted the similarity, Martin confessed to the crime. That's the nature of confession. Confession is simply identifying ourselves as the culprit.[9]

Conviction is never fun. The very word itself conjures up images of nasty jail cells and dangerous cellmates. Indeed, conviction is painful and we cringe at the prospect. But it's the first step toward confession. And without confession, we never escape the consequences of sin.

Confession of Sin

[2] Wash me thoroughly from my iniquity. Cleanse me from my sin. [3] For I know my transgressions. And my sin is ever before me. [4] Against Thee, Thee only, I have sinned. And done what is evil in Your sight. So that thou art justified when Thou dost speak. And blameless when Thou dost judge. Psalm 51:2-4 (OLD NASB)

As a youth minister in one of my first church jobs, I had a student named Gary who loved to write songs on his guitar. He was pretty good at it, too. My favorite was actually a rendition of the words from Psalm 51:2-4. As you probably know, David wrote Psalm 51 after the prophet Nathan confronted him about his adultery with Bathsheba and the subsequent murder of her husband. In Psalm 51, David pleads for forgiveness. Gary put those words to music using minor chords. I don't know how David's original version sounded, but Gary's was hauntingly beautiful. Sometimes I still sing it to God when I'm confessing my sins.

Unfortunately, we avoid confession like the plague. Perhaps because we see God as the ultimate cop, anxiously waiting to dispense justice and not in a good way. Like the cowboy who misjudged a curve and wrecked his pick-up truck, while pulling a horse trailer with his dog in the truck bed. When a state trooper arrived on the scene, he first found the horse in terrible shape and, drawing his pistol, he put the horse out of its misery. Bang! Next, the trooper found the dog in a similar state and put the dog out of its misery, too. Bang! Finally, the trooper found the cowboy who'd been thrown from the truck. The cowboy had three broken ribs, a huge gash in his forehead, and other internal injuries. The trooper approached the cowboy and asked, "Are you alright?" Seeing that the gun was still in the trooper's hand, the cowboy answered, "I never felt better in my life, officer!"[10] Sometimes we're like that cowboy. We try to hide the true state of our hearts because we're afraid of God and what He might do if we tell the truth about ourselves.

In his book on prayer, Philip Yancey says our "image of God, more than anything else determines our degree of honesty in prayer."[11] If we focus solely on His holiness, we'll expect only judgment from Him. In that case, our fear of judgment will prevent us from being honest with Him about who we really are. We'll forget that God loves us and is willing to forgive us. According to Yancey, "we must trust God with what He already knows,"[12] because "more than anything else, God wants [our] authentic self."[13] In fact, Yancey says that hiding from God may be what displeases Him the most.[14]

So how do we come out of hiding? Where's a good place to start our confession? I recommend the seven deadly sins – pride, envy, lust, sloth, greed, gluttony and anger. Or if you like "old school," how about the Ten Commandments? Do you have any gods before Him? Are there any "idols" in your life? Do you take His name in vain? Do you remember to keep the Sabbath day holy? Do you honor your father and mother? Do you murder people by harboring hatred in your heart? Do you commit adultery with lust in your heart? Do you steal, bear false witness or covet? If you can get through the seven deadly sins and Ten Commandments unscathed, you're probably just deceiving yourself. You're missing what Yancey calls the most important part of prayer – allowing your true self to be loved by God.[15]

Cleansing from Sin

If we confess our sins, he is faithful and just to forgive our sins, and to cleanse us from all unrighteousness. 1 John 1:9 (KJV)

The Bible is very clear. When we make Jesus our Lord and ask God to forgive our sin, God never sees us the same way again. When God looks at us, He sees Christ because we are clothed in the robes of His righteousness. From that day forward, we are free from the penalty of sin.

But I noticed something about the description of the bronze laver in the Scripture. I noticed that the priests used it to wash their hands and their feet. And that reminded me of what Jesus did the night before His death. On that night, Jesus took a towel and wrapped it around His waste and began to wash the feet of His disciples. This was unthinkable to the disciples, especially Peter, because washing feet was reserved for the lowliest servant. Only the lowest servant was required to wash feet. And yet Jesus, the One they believed to be the very Son of God, was washing their feet. When Jesus came to Peter, Peter tried to stop Him. In response, Jesus told Peter that unless He washed Peter's feet, Peter had no part with Him. In typical fashion, Peter then asked Jesus to wash his entire body. Jesus refused, saying you're already clean. I just need to wash your feet.

That scene is a great description of our spiritual condition after salvation. We're washed in the blood of the Lamb, but there are parts of us that need cleansing from time to time. Salvation means that God will not hold our sin against us when we reach heaven's gate. But in this life we tend to get dirty. We "pick up" things we shouldn't and get our hands dirty. Our feet get dirty, too. We walk where we shouldn't and step in stuff.

Confession is necessary because we don't just need to die forgiven, we need to live forgiven. Confession is the way we present our "hands" and "feet" to Christ. It's the way we come clean and escape from hiding. In the words of Yancey:

> Prayer invites me to bring my whole life
> into God's presence for cleansing and

restoration. Self-exposure is never easy, but when I do it I learn that underneath the layers of grime lies a damaged work of art that God longs to repair.[16]

Through confession, God restores His work of art. He does so by cleaning off the dirt and grime we collect as we walk through this world.

In Alcoholics Anonymous, they say that we're as sick as our secrets. When we confess those secrets to God (which were never a secret to Him in the first place), something amazing happens. We discover that our God is faithful and stands by His promise in 1 John 1:9. He forgives our sins and cleanses us from all unrighteousness.

That's the best part of confession. When we come clean, He makes us clean and sets us free from the condemning power of sin. Like the priests who stood before the bronze laver, we see ourselves as God sees us. First, as sinners in need of forgiveness. Then, as works of art restored to His original intention.

Summary

We love to hide our sin from ourselves and from God. Whether it's a pitchfork in the middle of the road or a robbery in the middle of the night, we don't like to admit our sinfulness. The laver teaches us that if you want to enter the Holy Place – if you ever hope to stand in the Holy of Holies – you must seek cleansing from a holy God, who is faithful to forgive.

Practical Suggestions

Using holy imagination, approach the bronze laver and look down at the water.

- Imagine the shimmer of the water above the reflective surface of the bronze bowl. Take a long look at who you see there.

- Ask God to reveal any sin that would prevent Him from hearing your prayers.

- Ask Holy Spirit to search your heart and your thoughts for anything that is separating you from God or impeding His work in your life.

- Be brave enough to confess those things and repent. Ask God for the will and the power to forsake them.

- Express thanks for His faithfulness to forgive. Praise Him for cleansing you from sin.

THE HOLY PLACE

Exodus 37:10-16 (HCSB) – The Table ¹⁰ *They made the table of acacia wood—two cubits long, a cubit wide and a cubit and a half high.* ¹¹ *Then they overlaid it with pure gold and made a gold molding around it.* ¹² *They also made around it a rim a handbreadth wide and put a gold molding on the rim.* ¹³ *They cast four gold rings for the table and fastened them to the four corners, where the four legs were.* ¹⁴ *The rings were put close to the rim to hold the poles used in carrying the table.* ¹⁵ *The poles for carrying the table were made of acacia wood and were overlaid with gold.* ¹⁶ *And they made from pure gold the articles for the table—its plates and dishes and bowls and its pitchers for the pouring out of drink offerings.*

Exodus 37:17-24 (HCSB) – The Lampstand ¹⁷ *They made the lampstand of pure gold. They hammered out its base and shaft, and made its flowerlike cups, buds and blossoms of one piece with them.* ¹⁸ *Six branches extended from the sides of the lampstand—three on one side and three on the other.* ¹⁹ *Three cups shaped like almond flowers with buds and blossoms were on one branch, three on the next branch and the same for all six branches extending from the lampstand.* ²⁰ *And on the lampstand were four cups shaped like almond flowers with buds and blossoms.* ²¹ *One bud was under the first pair of branches extending from the lampstand, a second bud under the second pair, and a third bud under the third pair—six branches in all.* ²² *The buds and the branches were all of one piece with the lampstand, hammered out of pure gold.* ²³ *They made its seven lamps, as well as its wick trimmers and trays, of pure gold.* ²⁴ *They made the lampstand and all its accessories from one talent of pure gold.*

Exodus 37:25-29 (HCSB) – The Altar of Incense ²⁵ *They made the altar of incense out of acacia wood. It was square, a cubit long and a cubit wide and two cubits high—its horns of one piece with it.* ²⁶ *They overlaid the top and all the sides and the horns with pure gold, and made a gold molding around it.* ²⁷ *They made two gold rings below the molding—two on each of the opposite sides—to hold the poles used to carry it.* ²⁸ *They made the poles of acacia wood and overlaid them with gold.* ²⁹ *They also made the sacred anointing oil and the pure, fragrant incense—the work of a perfumer.*

CHAPTER 5

INTERCEDING FOR OTHERS

W e come now to the first room within the Tabernacle itself. It was called the Holy Place and measured 30 feet by 15 feet. According to the description in Scripture, the Holy Place was basically solid gold. The walls were covered in gold. The "furniture" and utensils were made out of gold. Even the curtains had gold thread in them. Can you imagine stepping into that room and being surrounded by gold? Although it had no windows, it must have been breathtaking. The light from the lampstand would have reflected off all the gold in the room. But the beauty and material value of the room wasn't why they called it the Holy Place. There were far more important reasons for calling it holy.

The word "holy" can mean many things. It can mean sacred, exalted, divine, venerated or worthy of worship. It can also describe something solemn or reverent as in a holy calling or a holy moment. The best definition, however, is derived from the Hebrew root. In its most literal sense, the Hebrew word for "holy" means "set apart." In other words, the Holy Place was a "set apart" place. It was a place of exclusion, separated by the walls surrounding the courtyard and the Tabernacle itself. Only the priests could enter the Holy Place and, even they were confined to specific times during the day.

So why did they call it the Holy Place? First of all, because it was the threshold to the Holy of Holies – the place where God's presence was revealed in a pillar of smoke by day and a pillar of fire by night. The place was holy because God is holy, "set apart" from everyone and everything in the universe. There's no one and no thing like Him. No one and no thing even comes close to being who and what God is! And for that reason, the Holy Place was "set apart."

But there's another reason for calling it the Holy Place. It was holy or "set apart" because it was a place of service. Each and every day, the priests entered the Holy Place to serve God and His people. The service that the priests offered in the Holy Place revolved around the three items of furniture found within it – the lampstand, the table of showbread, and the altar of incense. The priests would serve at the lampstand by filling the lamps with oil and trimming the wicks. They'd serve at the table by tending to the bread and wine. And they'd serve at the altar by burning incense and sprinkling blood from the animal sacrifices.

When I first started visiting the Holy Place in my prayer time, I focused on the three items in the room and what they might be saying to us about God, Jesus, and the Trinity. The following chart is a summary of how each item reveals who God is.

The Holy Place			
	Lampstand	**Table of Showbread**	**Altar of Incense**
God	Revealer	Provider	Consuming Fire
The Trinity	The Father (of Lights)	The Son (Bread/Wine)	The Holy Spirit (Prayer Partner)
Jesus	The Light of the World	The Bread of Life	Our Intercessor

First, they speak about God as revealer (the lampstand), as provider (the table of showbread), and as a consuming fire (the altar of incense). Second, they represent each person of the Trinity – the Father of Lights (the lights of the lampstand), the Son (the bread and wine on the table), and the Holy Spirit (the smoke rising from the altar). Finally, they speak about Jesus as the light of the world (the lampstand), the bread of life (the table of showbread), and our intercessor (the altar of incense).

All of that was good, but I wasn't satisfied. I knew I was missing something. I just couldn't put my finger on it. The breakthrough came when I realized that the Holy Place was set apart *for service*. Just as the priests served God's people in the Holy Place, we are to serve other people in the Holy Place. In other words, the prayers we offer in the Holy Place should be a service to others.

Many books on prayer talk about the different types of prayer – meditation, thanksgiving, praise, consecration, confession, intercession, and petition. As we've traveled the Tabernacle path of prayer we've incorporated many of those aspects. Thus far, we've spent time outside the walls in stillness, solitude and silence. That's meditation. Passing through the gate, we've offered thanks for what God has done and praise for who He is. That's thanksgiving and praise. At the bronze altar, we've offered Him our very life and our love. That's consecration. And at the bronze laver, we've confessed our sin. That's confession. See where I'm going? The next type of prayer is intercession. The Holy Place is where we intercede for others. And each of the items in the

Holy Place are guides for our intercession. The lamp-stand, the table, and the altar of incense remind us of the people we should pray for and what we should pray for them.

The Lampstand

The Lord is not willing that any should perish. But that all should come to repentance. 2 Peter 3:9 (NKJV)

[37] Then he said to his disciples, "The harvest is plentiful but the workers are few. [38] Ask the Lord of the harvest, therefore, to send out workers into his harvest field." Matthew 9:37-38 (NIV)

At the lampstand, we remember that many people still walk in darkness and that God is not willing for any to perish (2 Peter 3:9). At the lampstand, we pray for God to shine His light into the hearts and lives of those who don't yet know Jesus Christ. We ask God to reveal Himself to them. We ask Him to convict them of sin and their need for forgiveness.

First, we pray for people we personally know who haven't made Christ their personal Savior and Lord. One of the best ways to identify those people within our particular spheres of influence is to use the acronym F.RA.N.K. It stands for Friends, Relatives, Associates, Neighbors and their Kids. We need to be frank with God about the FRANKs in our lives.

Second, after praying for people we personally know, we shift our focus to the rest of the world. The fields are still ripe for harvest and Christ still commands us to pray for that harvest. We pray for the missionaries already in the field. We pray for people groups who have yet to be reached. And we pray for God to raise up more workers for the harvest.

Praying for the lost is one of our greatest responsibilities as followers of Christ. It's a great responsibility because their need is great. It's a great responsibility because every person deserves to hear about Jesus. And it's a great responsibility because our great God both desires and deserves to be known.

The Table

And my God shall supply all your needs according to His riches in glory. Philippians 4:16 (NASB)

[P]ray for each other so that you may be healed. The prayer of a righteous person is powerful and effective. James 5:16 (NIV)

At the table, the bread and drink offerings remind us that God is the ultimate provider. Everything we need, He can provide. God is able to provide whether the need is physical, spiritual, emotional, financial, social, etc. No matter the size of the need, God is our source and He's able to supply (Phil 4:16). No need is too small for God to be concerned. And no need is too big for God to handle.

At the table, we intercede for the needs of others. Some like to use a prayer list of people in need. Others prefer to let God prompt their prayers by bringing different people to mind during their prayer time. Still others, organize their seasons of intercession around different types of needs – those with health issues, those who are grieving, etc. Regardless of the method, the table is where we pray for the specific needs of people we know and love.

The table is the place to pray for others, whether lost or saved, who are in need of the Lord's provision. According to James 5:16, the prayers of the righteous are effective. But they can only be effective if we pray. According to Scripture, Jesus prayed for others and He's still praying for us today (*see*, John 17; Romans 8:34). The table is where we join our prayers with those of Christ.

The Altar of Incense

May my prayer be set before you like incense; may the lifting up of my hands be like the evening sacrifice. Psalm 141:2 (NIV)

The altar of incense was a unique place of service in the Holy Place. In addition to making sure that the incense was kept burning, the priests had another duty to perform at the altar. Every day, the priests would sprinkle blood from the daily sacrifices upon the altar of incense. In essence, they presented the peoples' sacrificial offerings at the very entrance to the Holy of Holies. In so doing, they took part in the process as representatives of the people who presented their sacrifices.

Similar to the priests, the altar of incense is where we ask God what part He wants us to play in the process of answering our intercessory prayers. Having asked God to bring people to salvation and to supply the needs of others, at the altar of incense we seek God's guidance and instruction about the job He has for us to do.

With respect to the lost, we ask God to make us sensitive to those around us who need Christ. We ask

Him to provide opportunities for us to tell FRANK about Christ. We pray for boldness when those opportunities come. And we pray for wisdom and grace to present the Gospel in the most appealing way. In short, at the altar of incense we pray for the lost to be saved *and* for God to empower our witness to them.

With respect to our intercession for those in need, we ask God to show us how we can serve them. We ask Him to reveal what we can do to meet their needs. We ask for wisdom to offer comfort and counsel. We don't just sit idly by and expect God to do what's in our power to do. We ask God to show us how we can join Him in His work.

Summary

The Old Testament priests entered the Holy Place to serve the Israelite people. Likewise, Jesus said that He did not come to be served, but to serve, and to give His life as a ransom for many (Mark 10:45). When we pray, we serve others through intercession. This is one of the most significant things we can or will ever do as believers – bringing the needs of others before the throne of grace.

Practical Suggestions

Since you are entering the Holy Place to serve others, imagine the faces of those you serve. Bring them with you into this sacred room.

- Begin by examining the objects in the room – the lampstand, the table, and the altar of incense. See the light reflecting off the walls. Touch the table. Smell the incense.

- Stand before the lampstand and pray for those who still live in darkness. Pray for the FRANKs in your life. Ask God to shine His light upon them. Pray for God to send witnesses into their lives. Pray for conviction of sin and receptive hearts. Next, pray for harvest around the world. Pray for missionaries and mission fields.

- Stand before the table and pray for those who are in need of God's provision. Ask God to bring them to your mind. When He does, be bold and specific in your requests. But remember to seek glory for the Giver, not just gifts for the ones in need.

- Stand before the altar of incense and pray for God to reveal the part He wants you to play in answering the prayers you've just prayed. Ask Him to grant wisdom and boldness for ministry to the lost and needy.

THE HOLY OF HOLIES

Exodus 37:1-9 (HCSB) *¹ Bezalel made the ark of acacia wood—two and a half cubits long, a cubit and a half wide, and a cubit and a half high. ² He overlaid it with pure gold, both inside and out, and made a gold molding around it. ³ He cast four gold rings for it and fastened them to its four feet, with two rings on one side and two rings on the other. ⁴ Then he made poles of acacia wood and overlaid them with gold. ⁵ And he inserted the poles into the rings on the sides of the ark to carry it. ⁶ He made the atonement cover of pure gold—two and a half cubits long and a cubit and a half wide. ⁷ Then he made two cherubim out of hammered gold at the ends of the cover. ⁸ He made one cherub on one end and the second cherub on the other; at the two ends he made them of one piece with the cover. ⁹ The cherubim had their wings spread upward, overshadowing the cover with them. The cherubim faced each other, looking toward the cover.*

Exodus 40:20-21 (niv) 20 He took the tablets of the covenant law and placed them in the ark, attached the poles to the ark and put the atonement cover over it. 21 Then he brought the ark into the tabernacle and hung the shielding curtain and shielded the ark of the covenant law, as the Lord commanded him.

CHAPTER 6

PETITIONING THE HOLY ONE

For we do not have a high priest who cannot sympathize with our weaknesses, but One who has been tempted in all things as we are, yet without sin. Therefore let us draw near with confidence to the throne of grace, so that we may receive mercy and find grace to help in time of need. (Hebrews 4:15-16 ESV)

Be anxious for nothing, but in everything by prayer and supplication with thanksgiving let your requests be made known to God. And the peace of God, which surpasses all comprehension, will guard your hearts and your minds in Christ Jesus. (Philippians 4:6-7 NASB)

We come now to the final stage of our prayer journey through the Tabernacle. Having passed through the gate of the courtyard and the curtain at the entrance to the Holy Place, we are now standing outside the final curtain before the Holy of Holies. This last barrier is embroidered with the image of cherubim, like those who guarded the gate to the Garden of Eden after the fall of Adam and Eve.

When Christ died on the cross, a similar curtain in the Temple was torn in two from top to bottom (Matthew 27:51). The tearing of that curtain was God's way of demonstrating that, by virtue of Christ's death, we now have direct access into His presence. The cost for our access was paid, once and for all, by the precious blood of the ultimate sacrifice – the Lamb of God, who takes away the sin of the world (*see*, Hebrews 10:10-14, 1 Peter 1:18-9 and John 1:29).

Standing on the threshold of the Holy of Holies, we are reminded that only the High Priest was allowed to enter this sacred space and even he could enter only one day of the year – the Day of Atonement. For the High Priest, parting the final curtain was an act of bravery, for on the other side of the curtain was the One like no other. He is the One whom the prophet Isaiah saw "high and lifted up" (Isaiah 6:1). The One serenaded by Seraphim with continuous praise, "Holy, Holy, Holy is the Lord of Hosts" (Isaiah 6:3, Revelation 5:8). This is the first great lesson of Scripture. GOD IS HOLY!!! Mere words are insufficient to describe that holiness, but A. W. Tozer comes close:

> God's holiness is not simply the best we know infinitely bettered. We know nothing like the divine holiness... To be holy He does not conform to a standard. He is that standard. He is absolutely holy with an infinite, incomprehensible fullness of purity that is incapable of being other than it is.[17]

Living in an age of cheap grace and surrounded by voices screaming for tolerance, we in the church have become desensitized to all manner of unholiness. What's worse, all too often we are willing participants in it. According to Tozer, the reason for this condition is the fact that "the Church has surrendered her once lofty concept of God and has substituted for it one so low, so ignoble, as to be utterly unworthy of thinking, worshipping men."[18] Perhaps only through the discipline of prayer can we regain what we have lost, what Tozer calls the knowledge of the Holy.

Like the High Priests of old, we should approach the Holy of Holies with a powerful sense of fear and trembling. Although we are recipients of God's grace, we must never forget the holy fierceness of the One with whom we have to deal. In this sense, fear of the Lord truly is the beginning of wisdom.

This Holy One is not the cuddly, cringing god of this age. He is not ignorant of our willfulness; nor is He amused by our brazenness. He cannot ignore it and He does not condone it. In short, God is not someone to be trifled with. He is the Holy One of Israel! He is the Lion of the tribe of Judah! He is the One seated on the white throne of judgment! Amen and amen!

Although our God is holy, it's important to remember that "holy" is *not* all He is. While seeking to avoid the cuddly caricature of God promoted by those who seek only to ease their conscience, we must never forget that God is loving. Indeed, He's not only loving, the Scripture tells us that He *is* love (1 John 4:8). Since love is an intrinsic part of His nature, God's love for us is both irrepressible and inexhaustible. He cannot and does not stop loving us.

This may be a poor way to explain it, but when I was a child I had two toys that I remember well for different reasons – a tin Jack in the Box and a stuffed toy clown, which I ingeniously named "Clowney." When I played with the Jack in the Box, I would turn a crank on the side and it would play a tune. At the risk of planting a song in your head that you won't be able to get out, the words to the tune are: "Round and round the mulberry bush, the monkey chased the weasel. The monkey stopped to pull up his socks. Pop, goes the weasel!" After some time turning the crank (but at any time during the tune), the lid would fly open, a clown would spring out of the box, and I would jump out of my skin. It always scared the livin' daylights out of me. Needless to say, I came to detest that song and, um, "dislike" clowns. Clowney, on the other hand, was memorable for a completely different reason. Clowney was brightly colored (red in back and yellow in front) with a rubber clown head smiling from ear to ear. Clowney was extremely soft and he was my buddy. On occasion, he'd take a snooze with me. I genuinely loved Clowney. (Truth be told, I still love him. I just don't know where in the world he is!) Clowney changed my opinion about clowns. I still have a healthy respect for them, but I no longer jump when I see one.

I realize my relationship with Clowney and the Jack in the Box are a silly illustration, but I do have a point. We need to get past the idea that God hides in wait, looking for the first opportunity to pounce on us in judgment. God is holy, but that doesn't mean He's angry or mean. Likewise, God is not such a softy that we should treat Him casually, like a buddy. God is love, but that doesn't mean He's a pushover. In short, the God waiting on the other side of the curtain in the Holy of Holies is both holy and loving. We dare not treat Him disrespectfully and we must not take Him for granted.

When we step into the Holy of Holies, we find a single piece of furniture. It was called the Ark of the Covenant. Yes, the same one that was the subject of the movie "Raiders of the Lost Ark." I'm ashamed to admit that I made that connection long before I made the connection between Noah's ark and this ark. Noah's ark was actually a place of safety. In fact, it was the only safe place if you wanted to survive the flood of God's judgment. In that respect, the Ark of the Covenant has some important lessons to teach us about the nature of God and our relationship with Him. Specifically, the contents of the ark and its cover speak volumes about both subjects.

The Contents of the Ark
(Jesus Carried out the Law)

For we do not have a high priest who cannot sympathize with our weaknesses, but One who has been tempted in all things as we are, yet without sin. Hebrews 4:15 (ESV)

According to Exodus 40:20, the ark contained only one thing – the tablets of the covenant law. We call the laws engraved on those tablets the Ten Commandments. Carved in stone, they symbolize the standard of perfection that God demands. Unfortunately, no person, except Jesus Christ, has ever been able to live up to those high standards.

The contents of the ark remind us that Jesus carried out the law in every respect. He satisfied their every demand. He fulfilled their every purpose. He filled them with meaning. But then, after carrying out the law in every respect, Jesus carried our sin to the cross (*see*, 2 Cor. 5:21). He willingly accepted the death penalty for our failure. As Paul put it, God showed His love for us in this way, while we were still sinners Christ died for us (Romans 5:8).

And that's why Hebrews 4:15 is such great news. In Christ Jesus, we have a new High Priest who can sympathize with our weaknesses. Why? Because He's been there. He was tempted in every way just like us. But what's even better, He never gave in to sin. He had (and still has) the power to overcome whatever we may face. He is the only High Priest who knows our struggles *and* has the power to defeat them.

The Cover of the Ark

(Jesus Covered the Law with Mercy)

Therefore let us draw near with confidence to the throne of grace, so that we may receive mercy and find grace to help in time of need. Hebrews 4:16 (ESV)

My favorite part about the Tabernacle is the cover on the Ark of the Covenant. It was called the mercy seat. I think that's awesome! Anyone with a healthy understanding of God's holiness, enters the Holy of Holies with fear and trepidation. He is Holy with a capital "H" and we are not. BUT, as we draw back the curtain that veiled off the Holy of Holies, the light from the lampstand strikes gold and we are dazzled by the mercy seat. Rightly anticipating judgment, we are greeted by mercy.

How is it that we are allowed to approach the Holy One, much less receive mercy and grace? Because Jesus not only carried out the law; He covered it with mercy. By virtue of the blood that Jesus Christ shed on the cross, we can be covered with mercy and grace. His blood covers our sin and makes mercy possible. Just like it says in the old hymn: "What can wash away my sin? Nothing.

Nothing but the blood of Jesus." As believers, we have access to God and an audience before Him because Jesus covers us with His robes of righteousness.

That's why Hebrews 4:16 implores us to draw near with confidence. Because we are drawing near to a throne of grace – the Father's lap! It's safe to approach Him. And it's safe to present our requests to Him. In response, we can expect to receive mercy and grace to help us in time of need.

The Confidence of Petition
(Jesus is our High Priest)

Be anxious for nothing, but in everything by prayer and supplication with thanks-giving let your requests be made known to God. And the peace of God, which surpasses all comprehension, will guard your hearts and your minds in Christ Jesus. Philippians 4:6-7 (NASB)

At this point, it should be obvious that the Holy of Holies is primarily a place of worship. We worship God because He is holy. We worship Him because He is merciful. We worship Him because He is gracious. We could spend hours just worshipping Him for each of His attributes. But the Holy of Holies is also a place of petition.

As a lawyer, I know a thing or two about petitions. In the legal profession, a petition is the first pleading filed in every case.[19] The petition tells the court and the defendant what the plaintiff hopes to get out of the lawsuit and why they are entitled to it. For example, the plaintiff may want a heart-felt apology, a bucket full of tears, and a boatload of money because the defendant was a jerk and plaintiff got his wittle feewings hurt. In other words, a legal petition is a "pleading" which asks for stuff. What's even more interesting is that the petition concludes with a "prayer for relief."

Having made it thus far on the Tabernacle path of prayer, it's appropriate for us to present our personal requests to God – our petitions and prayers for relief. It's appropriate because our needs should rightfully come last. According to Philippians 4:6, it's also appropriate because God doesn't want us to be anxious about anything. He wants us to make our requests known to Him. He wants us to trust Him with everything. Because when we trust God with everything, we receive a peace from Him that's beyond comprehension (Philippians 4:7). He grants us peace that guards our hearts and minds, regardless of whether or not our specific requests are granted.

Summary

The Holy of Holies is the place we encounter God in all His holiness, mercy and grace. It's a place of worship and petition. It's the final and most important part of prayer because the Holy of Holies is the place we enjoy our personal relationship with Almighty God.

Practical Suggestions

We began this journey of prayer with the idea that prayer is where our personal relationship with God takes place. As you enter the Holy of Holies, consider the only object in this sacred space. Meditate for a moment on what it says to you about God and Jesus Christ.

- Open the Ark and look inside. Pick up the stone tablets etched with the Ten Commandments. Reflect on the burden of the law. Thank Christ for bearing that burden all the way to the cross.

- Close the cover and think about the mercy seat. The value of the gold in it is nothing compared to the price Christ paid for you to receive mercy. No wonder the cherubim are bowing over the mercy seat. Praise Christ for shedding His blood and paying the price so you can have a relationship with God the Father, God the Son and God the Holy Spirit.

- Now is the time to present your personal requests to God. Let Him know what you need. Hold nothing back. Trust Him with everything. Wait for the peace of God. Let it guard your heart and mind from fear and anxiety.

- Lastly, thank Him for answers you have received to previous requests.

Our prayer journey through the Tabernacle is now complete. So how do we leave? The same way we came in. We conclude our season of prayer with praise and thanksgiving.

CHAPTER OUTLINES, SCRIPTURE PROMPTS, AND PRACTICAL SUGGESTIONS

The Tabernacle Walls – Pulling the Curtains of Secrecy

<u>Slow Down (Stillness)</u> – *Be still, and know that I am God; I will be exalted among the nations, I will be exalted in the earth.* Psalm 46:10 (ESV)

<u>Shut Out (Solitude)</u> – *"And when you pray, you must not be like the hypocrites. For they love to stand and pray in the synagogues and at the street corners, that they may be seen by others. Truly, I say to you, they have received their reward. But when you pray, go into your room and shut the door and pray to your Father who is in secret.*

And your Father who sees in secret will reward you." Matthew 6:5-6 (ESV)

Hush Up (Silence) – *"And when you pray, do not heap up empty phrases as the Gentiles do, for they think that they will be heard for their many words. Do not be like them, for your Father knows what you need before you ask him."* Matthew 6:7-8 (ESV)

Using holy imagination, consider the white linen walls that separate the Tabernacle from the people.

- Pick a time and place for secret prayer and stick to it. Wherever and whenever it is, God will make it sacred.

- Do whatever is necessary to avoid interruption or distraction – shut the door, close the curtains, turn off the computer, silence the phone, etc. (You'll soon learn what needs to be done because the first few times, at least, you will be interrupted and/or distracted.)

- Remember the lessons of the Tabernacle walls – stillness, solitude and silence.

- Begin with Scripture. Read, recite, or just recall a verse that helps you settle yourself and get focused. For example, Psalm 46:10 or Isaiah 40:31.

- As you begin the season of prayer, envision the white linen walls of the Tabernacle courtyard. Imagine pulling them around you like curtains, shutting out the distractions of the world. Listen for the sheer sound of silence.

- Once you've spent enough time to experience "the peace of God which passes understanding," proceed to the gate.

The Gate – Entering the Gate

Give Thanks – *Enter His gates with thanksgiving and His courts with praise. Give thanks to Him and praise His name.* Psalm 100:4 (HCSB)

Adore Him – Psalm 100:4 above.

Take Time to Worship – *But You are holy, enthroned on [inhabiting] the praises of Israel.* Psalm 22:3 (HCSB)

Enter the Gate – *⁷So Jesus said again, "I assure you: I am the door of the sheep. ⁸All who came before Me are thieves and robbers, but the sheep didn't listen to them. ⁹I am the door. If anyone enters by Me, he will be saved and will come in and go out and find pasture. ¹⁰A thief comes only to steal and to kill and to destroy. I have come so that they may have life and have it in abundance.* John 10:7-10 (HCSB)

Approach the Tabernacle gate and enter the courtyard.

- Give thanks to God for things He has done for you recently and in the past – opportunities he has given you, people he has placed in your life, circumstances He has orchestrated to bless you, etc. Thank Him for both material and spiritual blessings.

- Praise God by focusing on a favorite attribute of His character. You may even want to read a chapter from Tozer's book, *The Knowledge of the Holy*.

- Take your time. Worship God in spirit and in truth for what He's done and for who He is.

- Find a hymnal and worship Him in song. Or, if you know a worship song by memory, sing it from your heart. (*Holy, Holy, Holy* and Chris Tomlin's *How Great Is Our God* are good options.)

- Reflect on Christ in the colors of the gateway tapestry – blue for His divinity, red for His humanity, white for His purity and purple for His royalty.

- After spending time in worship, imagine yourself walking through the gate into the Tabernacle courtyard.

The Bronze Altar – Laying Your
Sacrifice on the Altar

<u>Lay Your Life on the Altar</u> – *23 And He was saying to them all, "If anyone wishes to come after Me, he must deny himself, and take up his cross daily and follow Me. 24 For whoever wishes to save his life will lose it, but whoever loses his life for My sake, he is the one who will save it."* Luke 9:23-24 (NASB)

I beseech you therefore, brethren, by the mercies of God, that you present your bodies a living sacrifice, holy and acceptable to God, which is your reasonable service. Romans 12:1 (NKJV)

<u>Lay Your Love on the Altar</u> – *28 One of the teachers of the law came and heard them debating. Noticing that Jesus had given them a good answer, he asked him, "Of all the commandments, which is the most important?" 29 "The most important one," answered Jesus, "is this: 'Hear, O Israel: The Lord our God, the Lord is one. 30 Love the Lord your God with all your heart and with all your soul and with all your mind and with all your strength.'" Mark 12:28-30 (NIV)*

Approach the bronze altar slowly and reverently.

- Feel the heat of God's holiness and love.

- Deny yourself. Present your body as a living sacrifice. Maybe even say aloud, "I am crucified with Christ."

- Express your love for God and offer Him your affections, your decisions, your thought life and your physical strength. Lovingly surrender yourself to Him. Submit to His will.
- Ask God to help you yield yourself. Ask Him to increase your love for Him.

The Bronze Laver – Confessing Your Sins

Consequences of Sin – *If I regard [cherish] iniquity in my heart, The Lord will not hear.* Psalm 66:18 (NKJV)

Behold, the Lord's hand is not so short that it cannot save; nor is His ear so dull that it cannot hear. But your iniquities have made a separation between you and your God, and your sins have hidden His face from you so that He does not hear. Isaiah 59:1-2 (NASB)

Conviction of Sin – *²³ Search me, O God, and know my heart; try me, and know my thoughts. ²⁴ And see if there be any wicked way in me, and lead me in the way everlasting.* Psalm 139:23-4 (KJV)

Confession of Sin – *² Wash me thoroughly from my iniquity. Cleanse me from my sin. ³ For I know my transgressions. And my sin is ever before me. ⁴ Against Thee, Thee only, I have sinned. And done what is evil in Your sight. So that thou art justified when Thou dost speak. And blameless when Thou dost judge.* Psalm 51:2-4 (OLD NASB)

Cleansing From Sin – *If we confess our sins, he is faithful and just to forgive our sins, and to cleanse us from all unrighteousness.* 1 John 1:9 (KJV)

Approach the bronze laver and look down at the water.

- Imagine the shimmer of the water above the reflective surface of the bronze bowl. Take a long look at who you see there.

- Ask God to reveal any sin that would prevent Him from hearing your prayers.

- Ask Holy Spirit to search your heart and your thoughts for anything that is separating you from God or impeding His work in your life.

- Be brave enough to confess those things and repent. Ask God for the will and the power to forsake them.

- Express thanks for His faithfulness to forgive. Praise Him for cleansing away your sin.

The Holy Place – Interceding for Others

The Lampstand – *The Lord is not willing that any should perish. But that all should come to repentance.* 2 Peter 3:9 (NKJV)

[37] Then he said to his disciples, "The harvest is plentiful but the workers are few. [38] Ask the Lord of the harvest, therefore, to send out workers into his harvest field." Matthew 9:37-38 (NIV)

The Table – *And my God shall supply all your needs according to His riches in glory.* Philippians 4:16 (NASB)

[P]ray for each other so that you may be healed. The prayer of a righteous person is powerful and effective. James 5:16 (NIV)

<u>The Altar of Incense</u> – *May my prayer be set before you like incense; may the lifting up of my hands be like the evening sacrifice.* Psalm 141:2 (NIV)

Since you are entering the Holy Place to serve others, imagine the faces of those you serve. Bring them with you into this sacred room.

- Begin by examining the objects in the room – the lampstand, the table, and the altar of incense. See the light reflecting off the walls. Touch the table. Smell the incense.

- Stand before the lampstand and pray for those who still live in darkness. Pray for the FRANKs in your life. Ask God to shine His light upon them. Pray for God to send witnesses into their lives. Pray for conviction of sin and receptive hearts. Next, pray for harvest around the world. Pray for missionaries and mission fields.

- Stand before the table and pray for those who are in need of God's provision. Ask God to bring them to your mind. When He does, be bold and specific in your requests. But remember to seek glory for the Giver, not just gifts for the ones in need.

- Stand before the altar of incense and pray for God to reveal the part He wants you to play in answering the prayers you've just prayed. Ask Him to grant wisdom and boldness for ministry to the lost and needy.

The Holy of Holies – Petitioning the Holy One

<u>The Contents of the Ark</u> – *For we do not have a high priest who cannot sympathize with our weaknesses, but One who has been tempted in all things as we are, yet without sin.* Hebrews 4:15 (ESV)

<u>The Cover of the Ark</u> – *Therefore let us draw near with confidence to the throne of grace, so that we may receive mercy and find grace to help in time of need.* Hebrews 4:16 (ESV)

<u>The Confidence of Petition</u> – *Be anxious for nothing, but in everything by prayer and supplication with thanksgiving let your requests be made known to God. And the peace of God, which surpasses all comprehension, will guard your hearts and your minds in Christ Jesus.* Philippians 4:6-7 (NASB)

We began this journey of prayer with the idea that prayer is where our personal relationship with God takes place. As you enter the Holy of Holies, consider the only object in this sacred space. Meditate for a moment on what it says to you about our God and Christ.

- Open the Ark and look inside. Pick up the stone tablets etched with the Ten Commandments. Reflect on the burden of the law. Thank Christ for bearing that burden for us all the way to the cross.

- Close the cover and think about the mercy seat. The value of the gold in it is nothing compared to the price Christ paid for you to receive mercy. No wonder the cherubim are bowing over the mercy seat. Praise Christ for shedding His blood and paying the price so you can have a relationship with God the Father, God the Son and God the Holy Spirit.

- Now is the time to present your personal requests to God. Let Him know what you need. Hold nothing back. Trust Him with everything. Wait for the peace of God. Let it guard your heart and mind from fear and anxiety.

- Lastly, thank Him for answers you have received to previous requests.

Our prayer journey through the Tabernacle is now complete. So how do we leave? The same way we came in. We conclude our season of prayer with praise and thanksgiving.

Endnotes

1   Mark Twain, *The Adventures of Huckleberry Finn*, Franklin: Franklin, 1986, 18.

2   Richard Foster, *Prayer: Finding the Heart's True Home*, San Francisco: Harper, 1992, 74.

3   John Ortberg, *The Life You've Always Wanted*, Grand Rapids: Zondervan, 2002, 77, 79.

4   *Ibid.*, 81.

5   Dallas Willard, *The Spirit of the Disciplines*, San Fransisco: Harper & Row, 1988, 160.

6   *Ibid.*, 84.

7   Gary D. Chapman, *The 5 Love Languages*, Chicago: Northfield Publishing, 2010.

8   Andy Cook, *The Search for God's Own Heart*, Grand Rapids: Kregel Publications, 2001, 19-20.

9   Raymond McHenry, *McHenry's Stories for the Soul*, Peabody, Mass.: Hendrickson Publishers, 2001, 55.

10 Cook, 31.

11 Philip Yancey, *Prayer Does it Make any Difference*, Grand Rapids: Zondervan, 2006, 44.

12 *Ibid.*, 42.

13 *Ibid.*, 41.

14 *Ibid.*, 44.

15 *Ibid.*

16 *Ibid.*, 42.

17 A. W. Tozer, *The Knowledge of the Holy*, New York: HarperOne, 1961, 104, 105.

18 *Ibid.*, vii.

19 In some jurisdictions, the petition is called a "complaint." If you've ever read the book of Psalms, you know that's an acceptable name for prayer, too.

9 781629 525853